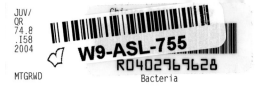

BACTERIA

Please visit our web site at: **www.garethstevens.com**
For a free color catalog describing Gareth Stevens Publishing's list of high-quality books and multimedia programs, call 1-800-542-2595 (USA) or 1-800-387-3178 (Canada). Gareth Stevens Publishing's fax: (414) 332-3567.

Library of Congress Cataloging-in-Publication Data

Invasion.
    Bacteria.
      p. cm. — (Discovery Channel school science. Universes large and small)
    Summary: Describes the appearance, characteristics, and behavior of bacteria, the most common lifeform on earth.
    ISBN 0-8368-3366-X (lib. bdg.)
    1. Bacteria—Juvenile literature. [1. Bacteria.] I. Title. II. Series.
QR74.8.I58   2003
579.3—dc21   2003042500

This edition first published in 2004 by
Gareth Stevens Publishing
A World Almanac Education Group Company
330 West Olive Street, Suite 100
Milwaukee, WI 53212 USA

This U.S. edition copyright © 2004 by Gareth Stevens, Inc. First published in 1999 as *Invasion: The Bacteria Files* by Discovery Enterprises, LLC, Bethesda, Maryland. © 1999 by Discovery Communications, Inc.

Further resources for students and educators available at www.discoveryschool.com

Designed by Bill SMITH STUDIO
Creative Director: Ron Leighton
Design: Eric Hoffsten, Jay Jaffe, Brian Kobberger, Nick Stone, Sonia Gauba
Production Director: Peter Lindstrom
Photo Editor: Justine Price
Art Buyer: Lillie Caporlingua
Print consulting by Debbie Honig, Active Concepts

Gareth Stevens Editor: Betsy Rasmussen
Gareth Stevens Art Director: Tammy Gruenewald
Technical Advisor: Sandya R. Govindaraju

Printed in the United States of America

1 2 3 4 5 6 7 8 9 07 06 05 04 03

© Juergen Berger/Max-Planck Institute/Science Photo Library/Photo Researchers, Inc.; p. 13, heat-loving bacterium, © Wolfgang Baumeister/Science Photo Library/Photo Researchers, Inc.; pp. 14–15, white blood cells ingesting bacterium, © Juergen Berger/Max-Planck Institute/Science Photo Library/Photo Researchers, Inc.; p. 20, E. coli, © Kwangshin Kim/Photo Researchers, Inc.; E. cloacae, © Oliver Meckes/Ottawa/Photo Researchers, Inc.; Proteus Mirabilis, © A. B. Downsett/Science Photo Library/Photo Researchers, Inc.; p. 21, Streptococcus, © Oliver Meckes/Ottawa/Photo Researchers, Inc.; white blood cells ingesting bacterium, © Juergen Berger/Max-Planck Institute/Science Photo Library/Photo Researchers, Inc.; Lyme disease bacteria, © M. Abbey/Photo Researchers, Inc.; p. 24, Antony van Leeuwenhoek, © Corbis-Bettmann; p. 25, Joseph Lister, © Corbis-Bettmann; p. 30, courtesy of Nancy Love.

Illustrations: pp. 16–17, map, Joe Le Monnier.

Writers: Barbara Ravage, Lynn Brunelle

Content Reviewer: Donald M. Silver, Ph.D.

Copy Editor: Joellyn M. Ausanka

Photographs: Cover, Tuberculosis bacteria, CNRI/Science Photo Library/Photo Researchers, Inc.; p. 2, E. coli, © Biophoto Associates/Science Source/Photo Researchers, Inc.; pp. 4–5, E. coli, © Biophoto Associates/Science Source/Photo Researchers, Inc.; E. coli (with pili) © CNRI/Science Photo Library/Photo Researchers, Inc.; thiocystis (with flagellum), © Alfred Pasieka/CNRI/Science Photo Library/Photo Researchers, Inc.; p. 10, plague bacterium, © CNRI/Photo Researchers, Inc.; p. 11, George Washington Carver, © Brown Brothers, Ltd.; p. 12, bacterium dividing, © A.B. Downsett/Science Photo Library/Photo Researchers, Inc.; flagella © CNRI/Science Photo Library/Photo Researchers, Inc.; Lyme disease bacterium,

BACTERIA

Bacteria. Ugh! They're bad for us, right? Well, actually, not all bacteria are bad. In fact, the great majority of them are friendly. More than 1,600 species of bacteria have been identified so far, and scientists are discovering new ones each day. Of those, only about 200 cause diseases in humans. Others are perfectly harmless to us, and many even help us.

Help? Sure, in ways that may surprise you. Bacteria help plants and animals grow. They help you digest your food. They even help fight disease, because many vaccines and antibiotics are made from bacteria. Some bacteria are responsible for making the food we eat, such as cheese, yogurt, and vinegar. Farmers use bacteria as fertilizers and for pest control. Bacteria can help clean up oil spills, industrial waste, and sewage.

There are more bacteria on Earth than any other kind of living thing. In fact, bacteria make life on our planet possible. In BACTERIA, Discovery Channel explains bacteria's long story to you. It goes back a few billion years, so make yourself comfortable. And be sure to wash your hands when you're through.

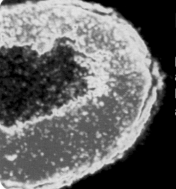

The age of human beings.
See page 9.

Final Project

BACTERIA

CYTOPLASM–The main ingredient inside each bacterium. It consists mainly of water and has a consistency like gelatin; the cell parts are suspended in it, like marshmallows or pieces of fruit.

Bacterium (singular), bacteria (plural): The word comes from the Latin meaning small "staff" or "stick." And it's true that some bacteria are shaped like sticks or rods. They're called bacillus bacteria. But other kinds look very different. Coccus bacteria are shaped like spheres. Spirillum bacteria are shaped like spirals.

Whatever their shape, all bacteria are one-celled organisms. They are so small that you cannot see them without a microscope, which is why they are called microorganisms or microbes.

The main difference between human cells and bacteria cells is that each of our cells has a distinct nucleus that contains complex genetic material. Human cells are surrounded by a membrane that allows certain molecules to pass through, while keeping others out. Bacteria cells don't have this same membrane-bound structure.

All bacterial cells are enclosed by a plasma membrane that keeps the inside in and the outside out. The innards always include cytoplasm, ribosomes, and a nucleoid. Some, but not all, bacteria also have a slime layer, cell wall, flagella, pili, and granules.

NUCLEOID–Not a true nucleus like human cells have. The nucleoid is a single DNA molecule that carries the genetic instructions passed from generation to generation of bacteria.

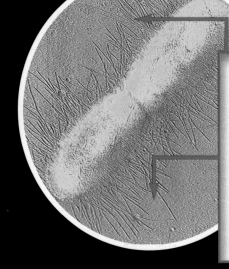

PILI–From the Latin word, pilus, for hair. Bacteria sometimes use these hairlike projections to adhere to other cells, often during an infection process. Also used to transfer genetic matter from one cell to another.

CELL WALL–Protective structure outside the membrane. It may be thin (one layer) or thick (two layers). Bacteria are often classified according to whether or not they have a cell wall and whether it's thin or thick.

PLASMA MEMBRANE–Surrounds the cell and separates it from the rest of the world.

FLAGELLUM–A whiplike structure that spins like a ship's propeller and helps the cell move through liquid environments. Some bacteria have one or more flagella, and others have none at all.

OTHER COMPONENTS

SLIME LAYER–An additional protective layer some bacteria have outside the membrane. It protects the cell from drying out and may be used to trap or hold other cells. On pathogenic (disease-causing) bacteria, it may help fend off attack from white blood cells inside the animals they infect.

GRANULES–Storage compartments for cell nutrients.

RIBOSOME–Ribosomes are the templates for making proteins. There are thousands of these floating in the cytoplasm of every bacterium.

THE BLACK DEATH

The first known outbreak of bubonic plague, or the Black Death, is recorded, killing a large percentage of the population. Medical historians today think it may have started even earlier, in the Himalayas bordering China and India.

Plague is caused by *Yersinia pestis*, a rod-shaped bacillus that is transmitted to humans in a particularly yucky way. *Yersinia* live in fleas, which settle into the warm fur of the common rat. When a flea bites a plague-infected rat, which it does quite often because rat blood is the flea's favorite food, it gets *Yersinia* in its meal. Eventually the rat dies of plague, and the flea looks for another home. If a rat is handy, it will choose the rat and pass along *Yersinia*. But sometimes a human is closer. But the same thing happens. A rat or a flea bites a human, the human gets *Yersinia*, and plague enters human blood. It continues to spread by flea bites or by inhaling bacteria when an infected person coughs.

So wherever you have rats and fleas—as if they aren't bad enough—there's a good chance you'll also have plague. And one place you're sure to find rats and fleas is in cities, where large numbers of people live close together. Between the 1200s and the 1700s, plague struck the cities of Europe with regularity. An estimated 20 percent of the population died of the disease during the plague years. One of the cities hardest hit was London in the mid-seventeenth century. It was one of the largest cities in Europe, and also one of the dirtiest. People lived crowded together in small houses that also played host to rats and fleas. In 1665 alone, plague killed as many as 7000 Londoners a week!

The names Black Death and bubonic plague accurately describe the symptoms. Usually within a few days—though it could be just a few hours—of being infected, the human immune system reacts by alerting the lymph glands that bacteria have invaded. The glands, which are distributed all over the body not far beneath the skin, scoop up the bacteria and swell into hard, pus-filled lumps called buboes ("byoo-bows"). The buboes often burst from the pressure, spewing the blood-blackened pus that has accumulated in them. Talk about gross! Blood leaks from broken vessels beneath, resulting in blackish bruises. Sometimes the lungs become infected. Then it's called pneumonic plague. Chills, fever, vomiting, and a rapid heartbeat are other symptoms of plague. Without treatment, more than half of those infected will die.

TO CURE THE PLAGUE

Long ago, no one knew what caused plague. They certainly didn't know how to prevent or cure it. Instead of information, they relied on superstition. Most people thought the Black Death was meant to punish people for sinful living of one sort or another. As for warding it off, they tried a collection of potions and magic charms.

Samuel Pepys (say "Peeps") kept a famous diary that tells us much about what day-to-day life was like in seventeenth-century London. Here are some of his impressions of plague-stricken London.

... To see a person sick of the sores, carried close by me by Grace-church in a hackney coach. ... To hear that poor Payne, my waiter, hath buried a child, and is dying himself. To hear that a labourer I sent but the other day to Dagenham's, to know how they did there, is dead of the plague; and that one of my own watermen, that carried me daily, fell sick as soon as he had landed me on Friday morning last, when I had been all night upon the water (and I believe he did get his infection that day at Brainford), and is now dead of the plague. To hear that Captain Lambert and Cuttle are killed in the taking these ships; and that Mr. Sidney Montague is sick of a desperate fever at my Lady Carteret's, at Scott's-hall. To hear that Mr. Lewes hath another daughter sick. And, lastly, that both my servants, W. Hewer and Tom Edwards, have lost their fathers, both in St. Sepulchre's parish, of the plague this week, do put me into great apprehensions of melancholy, and with good reason. But I put off the thoughts of sadness as much as I can, and the rather to keep my wife in good heart and family also.

"RING-AROUND-THE-ROSIES"

Some people believed that holding up flowers to the nose protected them from the bad air they thought caused the plague. They would dance in a circle with flowers singing "Ring around the Rosies/a pocket full of posies." But the song told the sad end of the story as well: "Ashes, ashes/All fall down [dead]."

Others wore charms such as dried toads and pouches of herbs around their necks. Another popular charm bore the magic word "abracadabra." From what we know now, a flea-collar would have been a better choice.

Some people chewed raw garlic and green walnuts. Perhaps they thought the smell and bitter taste would ward off the disease.

Many people smoked pipes and sat around smoky fires, believing that the smoke purified the air.

Today we know that the best way to avoid plague is to control rat and flea populations. For people who catch plague, strong antibiotic medicines will cure 95 percent of all cases.

Activity

CHARMED, I'M SURE A mysterious illness has stricken your school. What are the symptoms? Give it a name. Then make up a chant, a song, or a dance, or design some magic charms and amulets to wear as protection, keeping the symptoms and characteristics of the illness in mind.

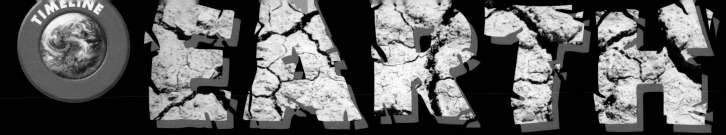

TIMELINE

EARTH

4.6 billion years ago	3.5 billion years ago	2.8 billion years ago	2.0 billion years ago	1.0 billion years ago

That's 4,600,000,000 years ago. (Some scientists say it was only 4.5 billion years ago. Whatever. We're talking about a really long time ago!) Hot gases, stardust, rock, and ice are pulled together into a roiling soup that eventually cools into what we now call . . . Earth.

The still-cooling rock is a mass of volcanoes, poisonous gases, steam, sulfur, and HOT, HOT, HOT water. Nothing could live in such a place, right? WRONG! Bacteria were apparently thriving. Recently, scientists discovered a kind of bacteria that thrives in the boiling waters of volcanic hot springs, a hostile environment resembling Earth of 3.5 billion years ago. Some scientists believe the first bacteria were similar to these. According to this theory, ancient bacteria absorbed hydrogen sulfide and gave off sulfur.

The first changes occur that will eventually make Earth's atmosphere hospitable to many forms of life. Bacteria, capable of using the energy in sunlight to make food (photosynthesis), give off oxygen as a by-product. As free oxygen enters the atmosphere, bacteria help make the planet livable, one tiny belch at a time.

The first cells with nuclei make their tentative appearance on Earth.

Millions of different life-forms make their debut, including fungi, green algae, and primitive marine plants.

BIRTH

400 million years ago	200 million years ago	160 million years ago	4 million years ago	Now
Plants spread out of water and onto land. The first trees sprout. Insects, including giant cockroaches, arrive on the scene.	Dinosaurs rule!	The first mammals appear.	Hominids—the ancestors of humans—appear and begin to walk upright.	It's the age of human beings. Bacteria are what got us here, and aren't we glad they came? We still need them for the air we breathe, the food we eat, and so much more.

Activity

US VERSUS THEM Split up into two teams, one representing bacteria, the other humans. Debate which has played a more important role in life on Earth.

Bacterial Good Guys

The Environmental Protection Agency says farmers in Arkansas and the other southern states can plant more Bt corn this year. Bt stands for *Bacillus thuringiensis*, a naturally made soil organism that produces a powerful but deadly protein. The organism is capable of killing the insect enemy of corn, the European corn borer, when ingested. U.S. farmers are thrilled. The corn borer has been eating its way through cornfields, to about a billion dollars a year in lost crops.

Unlike many pesticides, Bt-corn has no effect on people and most insects. But nothing's perfect: When the corn's pollen scatters in the wind, it lands on other plants, including milkweed. It just so happens that milkweed is the favorite food of monarch butterflies. When the monarchs eat milkweed touched by the pollen, almost half of their larvae are killed.

So Bt corn is good for corn growers and consumers, because increased production means cheaper corn at the supermarket. But it's definitely bad for butterflies.

Got You Covered!

We're covered with bacteria! Literally. If this gives you the creeps, rest assured. A huge army of beneficial bacteria patrol our skin and our intestines. It forms a protective barrier against invasion by harmful (pathogenic) bacteria, fungi, and other disease-causing organisms. Without that barrier, we'd be in big trouble.

Beneficial bacteria in our digestive tract make up what is called our normal flora. They can be found from one end—our mouth—to the other. The greatest number—trillions of bacteria of more than 500 species—live in the large intestine. Their main job is to break down nutrients into a form our bodies can use.

They also keep pathogenic bacteria in check, mostly by crowding them out and hogging all the food. But sometimes an infection won't budge. Antibiotic medicine usually takes care of the infection, which is good. But medicine strong enough to kill pathogenic bacteria often depletes the "good guys"— the normal flora—nearby. That upsets the balance of power and as a result, you may end up with another infection.

Or Are They?

Oil's Well That Ends Well

A huge oil spill occurs and the environment is threatened. What to do? Bring in the bacteria! Some species thrive in environments that would kill the rest of us: gas tanks, sulfur clouds, flows of boiling lava. Some bacteria "eat" oil spills. Others absorb poisonous gases and give off harmless ones. Some bacteria can help break down trash so landfills won't be a problem in the future. Lucky for us. Without their help, we'd soon be up to our armpits in garbage.

Alabama, U.S., 1898

Farmer and scientist George Washington Carver's experiments with peanuts make them a nutritional staple in the United States. Bacteria like them too. Legumes, a group of plants that include peanuts, peas, and beans, have little bumps, or nodules, in their roots. The nodules are home to *Rhizobium*. *Rhizobium* can absorb nitrogen gas from air pockets in the soil and convert it to nitrate, an essential nutrient in a form that plants can use. It works so well that legumes are often planted in fields every few years to renew nitrogen-depleted soil where other crops have grown. In this root/bacterial arrangement, everybody wins. Plants get the nitrogen they need to grow. Bacteria get a safe place to live. And humans get nitrogen-enriched soil in which to grow a variety of crops, not to mention all those peanuts!

Copenhagen, Denmark, 1935

Vitamin K is discovered, and you should be glad. The letter K comes from the Danish word for coagulation, which describes what this vitamin does. It helps blood clot and form scabs so the merest cut doesn't make us bleed to death. There are food sources of vitamin K, including spinach, kale, egg yolk, and liver. Not your favorite foods? Never fear! Enough vitamin K is manufactured in your large intestine, thanks to "good guy" bacteria that live there as part of your normal flora.

Activity

START YOUR OWN SCRAPBOOK Collect ads, articles, and pictures from newspapers and magazines. Include artwork (or make some of your own) and information about bacteria wherever it can be found: in the environment, in the lab, in our food, and in our bodies. The spotlight is usually on disease-causing bacteria, but see how much information you can gather about bacterial "good guys."

It Really Adds Up

How do bacteria make more of themselves?

First, the cell makes a copy of its DNA or its RNA molecule. Then it stretches into an elongated shape, narrows in the middle, and finally splits in half. Each half is equipped with its own identical copy of DNA or RNA. The result is two identical cells, called "daughters." Of course, by then the mother is history. The process is called binary fission, and it's really pretty simple, and fast! Some bacteria do it three times an hour. One bacterium becomes two; next thing you know, there are four, then eight, then sixteen, then . . . you get the idea.

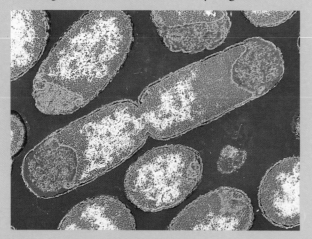

How Small is Small?

Bacteria are tiny. As tiny as the period in this sentence? Think again! The average bacterium measures between 1 to 10 micrometers. What's a micrometer? That's 1/1000 millimeter, or 1/250,000 inch. So it's clear you can't see the average bacterium without a microscope.

Bacteria tend to live in colonies, however, and when a lot of them cluster together—on a petri dish, for example—you can see the colony with the naked eye. It will look like a little mound.

They Get Around

How do bacteria get from one place to another?

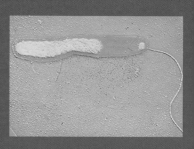

Some are able to move on their own, with one or more flagella— those little whiplike parts. They can move forward, toward something that attracts them, or away from something they want to avoid. The flagella spin like propellers. Spin one way, and the bacteria move forward. Spin the other way, and the bacteria just hang out, spinning around in one place.

Other bacteria need to be carried from one place to another:

▶ Some ride ocean tides, rushing rivers, and other moving bodies of water. The bacterium that causes cholera is waterborne.

▶ Some travel on currents of air, like the bacterium that causes tuberculosis. When an infected person coughs, sneezes, or even laughs, droplets containing bacteria are sprayed into the air and may be breathed in by others.

▶ Some hitch rides on fellow animals. *Borrelia burgdorferi*, the bacterium that causes Lyme disease, travels inside the deer tick, a tiny bloodsucker that feeds on warm-blooded animals. The tick passes the bacterium around to deer and mice, which don't get sick from it, and to humans, who do.

▶ There are even bacteria that use magnetism to get them going. These bacteria carry particles of iron in their cytoplasm, which orients them in terms of Earth's magnetic field.

One-Day Evolution

If you think of all the history of Earth as a twenty-four-hour day:

Midnight: Earth begins to form.
All through the night, Earth gradually cools.

5:30 A.M.: The day dawns and with it the age of bacteria.
All through the day, other microscopic forms of life develop, but it's well past dinner before you can see a living thing.

9:00 P.M.: The first trilobites and jellyfish show up on Earth.

11:00 P.M.: The age of the dinosaurs.

11:30 P.M.: Mammals appear.

11:59 P.M.: Just a few seconds before midnight, human beings arrive.

Bacteria are EVERYWHERE!

If you traveled to the farthest corner of Earth or even to the deepest part of the ocean, you'd find bacteria there. In the billions of years they've been on Earth, these tiny survivors have evolved and adapted to every one of Earth's environments.

Some scientists divide bacteria into two sub-kingdoms—Archaebacteria and Eubacteria. Archaebacteria live in extreme environments, such as active volcanoes, and are thought to be descended from the earliest bacteria. (Archae means "ancient"; it's the same root you see in archaeologist.) Eubacteria make up the second kingdom. Even though "eu" means "good," pathogenic bacteria are members of this kingdom too.

Many bacteria live in habitats you wouldn't dream of. Ice? No problem. Hot springs? Mmmm, love that heat! You're just as likely to find them in the desert as in the rain forest.

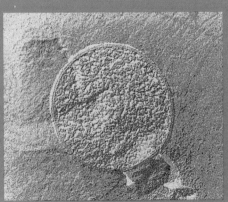

Many bacteria are anaerobic, which means they don't even need air to survive. In fact, a breath of fresh air will kill them. *Thermoacidophilus bacteria,* an archaebacterium that thrives on sulfur, has been found in hydrothermal vents on the ocean floor. The name means heat (thermo) and acid (acido) lover (phil). Another favorite habitat is underground—in the soil and in the roots of plants. And don't forget the human body. A stunning 100 trillion bacteria live in the average healthy human.

Activity

MICROBE MATH Suppose a cell divides every fifteen minutes. How many would there be by the end of the day? You do the math, but here's a hint: Think BILLIONS!

THIS MEANS WAR!

It's hard work being a pathogenic bacterium. In order to harm us, it first has to get inside our bodies. Then it must outmaneuver our immune system. Let's follow it and see what happens.

1. **Lucky break:** You've cut yourself on the sharp edge of a piece of paper. Unbroken skin is a very strong barrier, covered with beneficial bacteria, small hairs, sweat, and oil. All these things block bacterial growth. But when there is a break in the skin, bacteria can slip through. There it goes.

2. **Multiplication game:** Remember binary fission? That single bacterium may be on a mission, but it's not too busy to reproduce itself. Soon a single cell becomes a crowd swimming through the blood

3. **Call the cops:** White blood cells are like police officers on the beat, sweeping the neighborhood for crooks. When they meet invading bacteria, they surround them and a battle begins. Often, the white blood cells win, and the bacteria are history.

4. **Pus is us:** Sometimes, though, the bacteria outnumber the white blood cells or are just too powerful. Then the bacteria win. How can you tell? Pus is a sure sign that this has happened, since it's made up of dead white blood cells.

5. **SOS (Send in Soap):** The white blood cell soldiers couldn't hold back the bacteria, so it's time to call in reinforcements: soap and antiseptic cream or ointment. And covering the infection with a bandage until the skin heals will help, too.

6. **Moving on:** Sometimes, though, the infecting army travels to other parts of the body. When that happens, stronger antibiotic medicine may be needed to knock out the invaders.

White blood cells munch away at bacteria.

Activity

DEFEND! Most bacterial invasions end quickly, thanks to our body's natural defenses. Besides cuts, think about some other ways that harmful bacteria get inside our bodies. What entry might they use? Make a drawing of one of those ways.

On the Move

Bacteria cause disease in humans the world over. War and the displacement of refugee populations, resulting in overcrowding and poor sanitation, all contribute to the spread of infectious bacterial diseases. But there's another feature of modern life that contributes just as much. Can you guess what it is?

If you said "air travel," you're right! In the days when people tended to stay in the place they were born, infectious diseases were more localized. Nowadays, immigration and leisure travel often mean people pack bacteria along with their suitcases.

This map of the world shows just some of the places where five bacterial illnesses have cropped up in recent years. Can you figure out what social, political, and/or environmental factors may have contributed to these outbreaks?

Legend:

- ⬤ *Vibrio cholerae* **Cholera**
- ⬛ *Borrelia burgdorferi* **Lyme disease**
- △ *Yersinia pestis* **Plague**
- ◇ *Escherichia coli* **Food poisoning**
- ⬡ *Mycobacterium tuberculosis* **Tuberculosis**

Activity

PLAN AHEAD You're planning a trip for your summer vacation. Pick a single destination or design a more complex itinerary. What bacterial illnesses might you find there? What should you do to try to protect yourself from getting sick?

I Just Can't Resist

Q: **You're an antibiotic. Anti means "against." What do you have against bacteria?**

A: Look, I've got no complaint with most of them. There are just a few I can't stand. Hate them with a passion. Want to kill them. We're sworn enemies. Even though we're related.

Q: **You are?**

A: Sure. Lots of antibiotics are made from bacteria or fungi (molds). The first antibiotic, penicillin, was scraped off some old moldy bread. But we've come a long way since then.

Q: **What do you mean?**

A: Now we come in a lot of different forms. We can be pills or capsules. We can be liquids. We come in shots when we need to get to work really fast—like when someone's really sick and doesn't have time for the pills to work. Just a little pinch and we're rushing into your bloodstream. And let's see—for skin infections, we come in creams

or ointments. There are even eye drops for bacterial infections in the eye.

Q: **Do you kill all bacteria or just certain kinds?**

A: Most antibiotics are called broad-spectrum. That means they can knock out many different types of bacteria.

Q: **That's good.**

A: No, that's bad. Because most bacteria are good. But we can't tell the good guys from the bad. All we can do is knock out everything. It's not our fault, but it can cause some real problems.

Q: **What kind of problems?**

A: Where should I start? Without your normal bacterial flora, you may get a stomachache or have trouble digesting food until the bacteria in your digestive tract begins to grow back. Other organisms, such as yeasts and other fungi, may take advantage of the space and food not taken up by your normal flora. They'll grow like wildfire, and you may end up with a "yeast infection." Antibiotics can also knock out the beneficial bacteria on your skin. The result might be a fungal infection like athlete's foot.

Q: **Yuck! Then what should we do?**

A: Only way to handle it is to take more medicine. That's one reason it's important to only take antibiotics for bacterial infections serious enough to risk these other problems.

Q: **You said one. Is there another reason?**

A: Yep. And it's really, really, really important. When antibiotics are used too often or used in the wrong way, bacteria develop something called resistance.

One of the main ways resistance happens is when people don't take all their medicine. They get through a few days, start feeling better, and don't bother to finish their medicine. Bad move.

Q: **But why take medicine after you're feeling better?**

A: Bad bacteria LOVE that kind of thinking! See, here's the deal. Antibiotics take a while to work—like about ten days. During the first few days, the weakest bacteria are killed off. But it takes more time to kill the strongest ones. So if someone stops taking medicine after only the weaker ones are gone, the strongest ones are still left. And guess what they do?

Q: **Hang around?**

A: Yes, but that's not all. They divide and multiply, and each one of their "daughters" inherits their strength. So you're actually creating a huge crowd of superstrong bacteria by not taking all your medicine—a huge population of resistant bacteria. Not only are you sick—and maybe even sicker than you were—but those bacteria can move on to another person, spreading resistance along with the disease.

Q: **Does that happen a lot?**

A: Unfortunately, yes. And it happens all over the world. We've had antibiotic medicines for a little over half a century, but in that time, some bacteria have developed resistance to just about every antibiotic invented. People are worried that soon we won't have any medicines to fight really serious bacterial diseases. And because we live in a very small world, resistant bacteria in a sneeze in the United States can travel all the way to China!

Q: **So what can people do?**

A: If your doctor prescribes antibiotics, take them all! Don't skip doses, and by all means, don't stop taking the medicine if you start feeling better.

Activity

ON THE AIR Make a poster or advertisement about antibiotic resistance. It could be a collage, a cartoon, or some other graphic. Or write a script for a TV or radio ad or news report. Include recommendations for fighting this threat to public health.

My, What a Handsome FAMILY!

These greatly magnified, color-enhanced creatures represent the three common bacterial forms: bacillus, coccus, and spirillum.

Enterobacterium cloacae is a common resident of the human colon.

E. coli is even more common in the digestive tract.

Bacteria that are rod shaped are called bacilli. They may or may not have cell walls and may or may not have pili or flagella.

BACILLUS

Proteus species also cause diseases of the digestive tract.

COCCUS

Bacteria that are globular are called cocci.

The prefix *stapho* means "cluster," so a staphlococcus is a cluster of globular bacteria.

The prefix *strepto* means "chains". So a streptococcus is a chain of globular bacteria.

SPIRILLUM

A bacterium that is helix-shaped is called a spirillum.

Borrelia burgdorferi causes Lyme disease.

Activity

THE NAME GAME Can you think of a good way to memorize these three different shapes of bacteria, and what they're called? Study the Latin words, bacillus, coccus, and spirillum, and come up with a foolproof way to know which is which. (Hint: Look closely at the letters of the names, and think how these might be related to the bacteria shapes.)

Petri Dish Puzzler

One of these bacteria caused a terrible disease, but which one was it?

Each of three scientists has a theory, but all of them are a little mixed-up. Each theory contains two statements, one that is true and one that is false. Can you figure out which bacterium is the culprit?

Scientist #1: "The microbe has pili and internal granules."

Scientist #2 : "The microbe is rod-shaped and it doesn't have any granules."

Scientist #3: "The microbe is gray and has no pili."

The answer is F. Since each scientist said one true and one false thing, any bacterium that had both or neither of the characteristics named by one scientist can be eliminated. From Scientist #1, B, C, D are eliminated. From Scientist #2: A, C, D are out. From Scientist #3, A, B, C, G, H get crossed off the list. That leaves F.

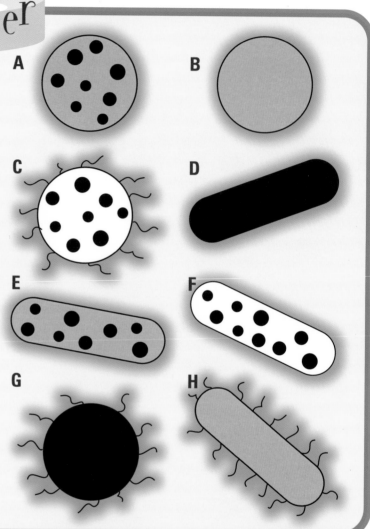

A   B

C   D

E   F

G   H

Rotten Riddles

Why did the bacteria cross the microscope?

To get to the other slide

What do you get if you cross a disease-causing bacterium with a comedian?

Sick jokes

Where do germs go for lunch?

A bacteria cafeteria

What's a bacterium's favorite health food?

Wheat germ

Where do bacteria go for vacation?

"Germ"-any

What was the name of the movie about prehistoric bacteria?

Germassic Park

Match the Microbes
Which two bacteria are exactly alike?

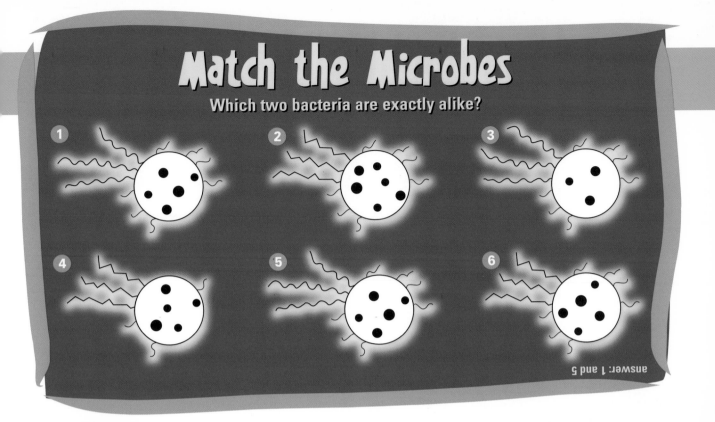

answer: 1 and 5

Activity

MAKE YOUR OWN BACTERIAL CULTURE (THEN EAT IT!)

Bacteria don't need much help when it comes to growing and multiplying, so making yogurt is easier than pie. You can do it at home or in the classroom. Here's what you'll need:

- a clean container: It should hold at least 8 ounces; almost anything will do—an empty yogurt or other plastic container, a glass jar, or a paper cup.
- a small box—a shoebox works well
- a sheet of foam rubber or a few handfuls of polystyrene foam pellets
- measuring cup
- measuring spoons
- store-bought plain, unsweetened yogurt: You'll need only a teaspoon per person, so a little goes a long way.

IMPORTANT: Read the label to make sure there are living bacteria in the yogurt. How can you tell? Look for the words "live yogurt culture," "acidophilus," or "lactobacillus."

- milk—it can be anything from skim to whole milk, though whole milk works best.
- optional—instant powdered nonfat dry milk—commercial yogurts are often thickened with a kind of edible seaweed or powdered milk.

Here's what to do:

1. The bacteria that make yogurt like a warm (not hot) and quiet environment to do their thing. Line the box with foam to make a cozy bed, and find a warm place to put it, away from the action. Near a radiator or a sunny window are good choices, but you may find others.

2. Bring the milk to room temperature and measure out 8 ounces.

3. Stir in 1 teaspoon of store-bought yogurt and 1 tablespoon of powdered milk, if you decide to use it.

4. Pour the mixture into the container and put it in its nest in the box. Cover with the box's lid, a sheet of clean paper, or a clean cloth (a dishtowel or washcloth will work fine).

5. Leave it alone! Do not peek, rattle, jiggle, or poke for at least 24 hours.

THE NEXT DAY: Is it yogurt yet? There's only one way to tell, so grab a spoon, stir in your favorite flavoring (try pieces of fresh fruit, jam or preserves, a bit of honey, chocolate syrup, a sprinkling of granola—whatever you like), and chow down.

Magnificent Microbe Moments

Bacteria have been here for billions of years, but it took humankind a long time to find out about them. First we needed the tools to study them. What we have learned about bacteria—what they look like, how they work, what effect they have on our lives and the world on which we live—is information gathered over less than 400 years. Let's turn the spotlight on some of the heroes in microbiology, the study of bacteria and other microscopic forms of life.

Delft, Holland, 1674

Antony van Leeuwenhoek (LAY-ven-hook), a maker of men's clothes, wants to closely examine fine fabrics. So he makes a powerful lens that can magnify things up to 300 times their size! This was not the first microscope, but it was more powerful than any that had been made before.

Leeuwenhoek starts looking at other things besides cloth. A hair from his beard . . . drops of blood . . . pond water . . . spit. He's amazed at what he sees: little animals. He calls them "animalcules," and today we call them one-celled organisms, or microbes.

Leeuwenhoek makes drawings of everything he sees. In 1674, he publishes his first report, which describes red blood cells. Later, he describes bacteria: bacilli, cocci, and spirilla.

Paris, France, 1862

French scientist Louis Pasteur is one of the most brilliant people of his time. He figures out that heating milk will kill the bacteria that cause it to spoil. The process, called "pasteurization," is still used today.

Later, Pasteur takes the germ theory a step further by developing a way to prevent bacteria from causing disease. It's called vaccination, and Pasteur discovers it by accident. He notices that bacteria weaken after a few generations and the weaker the bacteria, the less likely they are to make people sick. Pasteur takes the daring step of injecting some very weak bacteria—the kind that causes rabies—into a boy who had been bitten by a dog with rabies. (Luckily for us all, the boy lives.)

Why does vaccination work? Even though the weakened bacterium won't cause illness, the immune system marks it as an enemy and puts it on the "most wanted" list. The next time the invader turns up in the body—it could be years later—the immune system spots it immediately and knocks it out.

Among the vaccines Pasteur has developed are those against the bacterial diseases anthrax, cholera, and diphtheria.

Germany, 1876

Robert Koch ("coke") picks up where Leeuwenhoek left off, by claiming bacteria could cause disease. But no one is buying this new "germ theory of disease." The doubters insist that tiny things like bacteria couldn't possibly sicken larger ones like people.

Koch says not only do bacteria cause disease, but specific bacteria cause specific diseases. He sets out to learn which bacteria are responsible for some of the world's deadliest diseases, going to Africa and India.

In 1876, he makes his first major discovery: Bacillus anthracis, the bacterium that causes anthrax, a devastating disease of sheep and cattle. He goes on to discover the bacteria that cause tuberculosis and cholera.

London, England, 1865

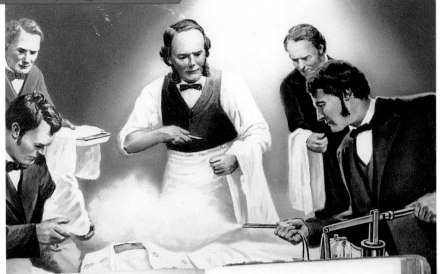

While Koch and Pasteur are investigating bacterial diseases, British surgeon Joseph Lister has another problem: His patients are dropping like flies! Even after successful surgery.

Lister believes the germ theory of disease and takes steps. His idea is to use carbolic acid, which he knows can kill bacteria, on everything that touches a patient during surgery. He sprays it on his scalpel and other instruments; he sprays his hands; he sprays the bandages. He even sprays carbolic acid directly in the wound.

And guess what? It works. The culprit is sepsis, infection caused by bacteria that get inside the body when the surgeon cuts through the skin. Before Lister started his antiseptic campaign in 1865, 50 percent of his surgical patients died. Afterwards, deaths were down to 15 percent. Today, patients are even less likely to develop a life-threatening infection as a result of surgery.

Germany, 1881

Fanny Hesse's microbiologist husband, Walter, has a problem: Bacteria in the lab are grown in a sort of broth, making it hard to see and study growing colonies. Walter says he needs something bacteria could grow on, not in.

In Fanny's kitchen is a substance called agar, which cooks used to make jams, jellies, and puddings. When dried agar is mixed with water, boiled for a while, and left to cool, it solidifies into a rubbery mass. Fanny suggests pouring it into a petri dish to have the perfect place to grow bacteria. It's still used for that today.

London, England, 1928

British chemist Alexander Fleming looks at some forgotten petri dishes in which he had been growing bacteria. They're useless. They've been exposed to the air and are probably contaminated by other microbes. In fact, they're covered with mold. He is about to toss them out when something catches his eye. Where there is mold, there is no bacteria. He soon concludes that mold has killed the bacteria.

The mold is penicillin, an extremely common fungus that grows on bread and other food, including agar. It can stop many kinds of pathogenic bacteria dead in their tracks by damaging the bacterial cell wall, which strips the cell of protection from the outside. It is the first antibiotic ever discovered.

Activity

MY FAVORITE MISTAKE Some of the most important scientific discoveries were made by accident. Write a journal entry, a short story, or a dramatic sketch about an accidental discovery you or someone your age has made. The situation can be fictional. It can even be funny. Just be sure to include the outcome: How did the accident change things?

25

THE MYSTERY OF THE

Poisonous Picnic

Every time you open your mouth to scarf down some lunch, an invisible cloud of bacteria swarms in along with your slice of pizza. Most of the time your body can handle anything that comes in. Stomach acid is strong and not a pretty place for bacteria to hang out. And your normal bacterial flora are taking up most of the space in your intestines, hogging most of the food. But sometimes dangerous bacteria do get in and survive. And then it's pure poison.

Marty and Sue Bailey had a great time at the Smiths' picnic, but later that night, Marty started feeling sick. By morning, he was vomiting and had a bad case of diarrhea. Sue was sorry to see her brother in such misery, but she was feeling fine. Mrs. Bailey called Dr. Wise, who said to bring Marty to the office right away. She brought Sue along just in case whatever was ailing Marty struck Sue next.

On the way to the doctor's office, Mrs. Bailey asked her children what they had eaten at the picnic. Let's listen in on their conversation.

Mrs. Bailey: Now, Marty, I want you to tell me everything you ate last night.

Marty: (between groans) I had potato chips, two hot dogs nice and charred like I like them, cola, and some carrot sticks.

Mrs. Bailey: How about you, Sue?

Sue: I had a hamburger, well done, some cole slaw, and pickles. And I drank some apple juice.

Mrs. Bailey: Hmmm. What kind?

Sue: I think the label said Big Apple Pure and Pasteurized.

Mrs. Bailey: Where was the cole slaw kept?

Sue: It was in a covered plastic container in the cooler. Mr. Smith said he was keeping it there so the mayonnaise in it wouldn't get all gross.

Mrs. Bailey: I wonder if Marty got sick first because he ate sooner than you did. I hope not, but you could be getting sick in a while too.

Sue: Thanks a lot, Mom!

Marty: Anyway, Mom, I ate a LOT later than Sue. That's why I had to settle for a hot dog. The burgers were all gone, and so were the paper plates.

Mrs. Bailey: Why were you so late?

Marty: A couple of the guys and I were catching salamanders in this muddy pool in the woods, and by the time we got back, everyone else had eaten.

Mrs. Bailey: Did you wash your hands before you ate?

Marty: (groans) Yes, Mom.

Mrs. Bailey: And you didn't get any of that water in your mouth.

Marty: (groans again) No, Mom.

Mrs. Bailey: OK, we're almost at the doctor's. If all the paper plates were gone, what did you put your food on? You didn't just carry it around in your hands, did you?

Marty: Course not. I found a plastic plate near the barbecue grill. I think they piled the burger patties on it before they were cooked. Anyway, no one was using it, so I did.

Mrs. Bailey: Well, here we are. Maybe the doctor can figure out what you have and how you got it.

Can YOU figure out what's wrong with Marty and how he got sick? Use the following safety tips and bacteria descriptions to solve the mystery.

Safety Tips

Clues

- Keep hot things hot and cold things cold.
- Cook all meat and seafood thoroughly.
- Wash fruits and vegetables, especially if they are to be eaten raw.
- When preparing raw meat, be sure all knives, cutting boards, and containers are washed thoroughly with soap and hot water before they are used for any other ingredient.
- Wash your hands before and after preparing food and before eating a meal.

Kinds of bacteria that produce food poisoning:

Escherichia coli: Called *E. coli* for short, breeds in hamburger meat and unpasteurized fruit juices.

Salmonella enteriditis: Breeds in poultry, especially chicken and eggs. Eggs are an ingredient in mayonnaise.

Shigella: Breeds in fresh vegetables.

(Answer on page 32.)

Activity

LUNCH TIME Your class is planning a picnic for the last day of school. It's June and the weather will probably be fine, if a little hot. What should you bring? How should the food be prepared and kept? Remember, you probably won't eat for at least four hours after the food leaves the kitchen.

Passing Mustard

Bacteriologists, like all scientists, use a certain process as they conduct their investigations. They follow certain steps, including hypothesis, observation, procedure, and results. See if you can follow the scientific process as Tim Take-Out, Professional Chef, attempts to pass mustard—er, muster—in the kitchen.

MONDAY, 6 A.M.

New restaurant job today. Get in early to see the kitchen. It's so disgusting, my tall hat wilted.

Hypothesis:

It looks to me like a teeming bacterial breeding ground. Of course, I can't actually see any bacteria teeming, but I know the signs.

Observation:

Bacteria traps everywhere. What a mess! Soggy sponges, damp towels, and blood-stained aprons (I sure hope that's beef blood). Puddles of old grease on the stove, sticky patches of who-knows-what on the floor. I can't believe my eyes: raw chicken on the counter, raw vegetables right next to it, unwashed knives, a pitcher of milk souring in the corner. To make matters worse, something is blocking the refrigerator door and I can tell from by how soft the butter is that the door has been open all night.

In short, a nightmare!

Make that a double nightmare. Ann T. Septic, the health inspector, is due around lunchtime. That gives me less than six hours to wipe out the bacteria and make sure it doesn't come back.

What I need is a plan:

Procedure:

► My materials: bleach, soap, and hot, hot water.

► Bleach kills bacteria, so I make a solution in a bucket of hot water and use it to swab the floor and the counters. Bleach and hot water in the sink, and in go the cutting boards, knives, and sponges.

► I gather up all the damp towels and grimy aprons and toss them in the washing machine, along with a cup of detergent and a cup of bleach. Then I spin the dial to "hot."

► Same with the dishwasher: mixing bowls, pitchers, measuring cups, what have you—it all gets the soap and hot water treatment.

Er, Muster

MONDAY, 9 A.M.

Results:

The kitchen looks spotless. But is it? I'll have to wait for the inspection to find out for sure.

In the meantime, I post a list of food safety rules:

1. **Treat Meat with Heat:** Cook all meats thoroughly; bacteria that thrive on raw meat can't take the heat.

2. **Cool It:** Store food in the refrigerator, and make sure the door is closed! Food-loving bacteria don't reproduce in cool temperatures. Better yet: freeze it.

3. **Pickle It:** Salt and vinegar make a hostile environment for many bacteria.

4. **Can It:** Bacteria cannot reproduce in the heated, then sealed, confines of a can or preserving jar.

5. **Dry It:** Take away the water where many bacteria thrive.

MONDAY, 12 NOON

Inspector Ann T. Septic arrives. Within half an hour, she's checked out the kitchen and pronounced it clean as a whistle. Whew!

As soon as she leaves, Tim sits down for lunch. He eats cheese on sourdough bread, olives, and frozen yogurt. What's funny about that?

Activity

SOMEONE'S IN THE KITCHEN

Tim Take-Out may be a professional chef, but he used the scientific method to pass the inspection. Now it's your turn. Armed with a clipboard and everything you've learned, pay a visit to your own kitchen. But this time, look at it in a different way. Using the scientific method, take a look around and write up your observations. Then draw your conclusions by grading your home kitchen on a scale of 1 ("Shut it down immediately!") to 10 ("Can't wait for dinner!") Remember to note both good and bad kitchen habits, food preparation, and storage conditions. And write your recommendations for improving anything that doesn't pass the test. Share them with your family—after dinner.

What a Waste!

Ever wonder exactly what happens to what goes down the drain? Nancy Love is an environmental engineer who studies and designs wastewater treatment plants. She told us that when it comes to human waste, bacteria make all the difference.

So what do bacteria have to do with sewage anyway?

Plenty! Bacteria take waste products and recycle them into products that won't poison the environment. In some cases, they create energy we can use. To bacteria, our waste is food.

Food? What do you mean?

The basic elements of sewage are carbohydrates, sugar, and fat. Bacteria love that. To them, it's candy. But the molecules are too big; they have to be broken into "bite-size pieces" before bacteria can take them in. It's kind of like if you saw a yummy ten-foot-long candy bar—you can't eat it in one bite.

If bacteria are everywhere and they eat our waste, why do we need sewage plants?

If we dumped sewage into a river, the bacteria would need to use lots of oxygen to break it down. The bacteria would use up all the oxygen in the river, and animals like fish would die because they can't get any. So it's important to do this process differently if we want our environment to thrive. Treatment plants make the process happen faster—we control the oxygen and time.

How do you do that?

My job has two sides. First, I have to give the bacteria the right environment so they can do their job quickly and effectively. Second, I have to figure out exactly what kind of waste material is coming down the pipe and how to arrange the treatment plant so that the right kind of bacterial "soup" develops to break down the waste material. Many plants have to treat industrial and human waste. Wastewaters that come from different places contain different things. For example, wastewaters from papermaking industries contain different chemicals than those from ice cream industries.

What do you do once the waste arrives at the plant?

It's an energy balance: the energy in wastewater is used to generate new bacterial cells, water, and gases, like carbon dioxide and nitrogen. Eventually, some of the bacterial cells have to be disposed of or else we would be up to our ears in bacteria!

After the Flush

Push the little lever and WHOOOSH! It's gone. Not your problem anymore, right? So where does it go?

▶ **Pump house:** Most sewage systems have a series of small pump houses that push the waste to the treatment plant. Try to find the pump houses in your neighborhood.

▶ **Treatment plant:** Do you know where the sewage treatment plant is in your city or town? More than likely, it's near a river or other body of water. Once sewage gets there, it follows a number of steps.

▶ **Filtering:** First, waste passes through a screen with half-inch holes in it. The filter sorts out all the big, nonwaste debris. People flush the most amazing things! Toys, rocks, rags, you name it.

▶ **Settling:** Next, it goes into a holding tank where gritty material that might damage the pipes is allowed to settle out—bone chips, egg shells, and sand, for instance. What's left is siphoned off and sent to the primary clarifier.

▶ **Clarification:** Solids are separated from liquids. The solids sink to the bottom and are raked off into a floor drain, while the water containing dissolved and small particles of waste, called colloids, is sent to the secondary treatment system. The solids are sent through a pipe to a different location in the treatment plant where solids are treated further.

▶ **Secondary treatment:** Wastewater is blended with bacteria and oxygen. The dissolved molecules and colloids are consumed and broken down by bacteria, and new bacterial cells, water, and gases are formed. After the liquid is treated by bacteria, the water that flows from the secondary clarifier is chlorinated to kill any bacteria that remain, then dechlorinated to make it safe for the environment. This treated water is released into a nearby river.

▶ **Solid treatment:** The solids that are collected during the wastewater treatment process have to be treated, too. In some cases, the solids are treated further by bacteria, which convert the food remaining in the solids into a soil-like solid residue and methane gas. The gas can be burned to generate electricity, and the solid residue can be applied to land as fertilizer.

Is your future teeming with bacteria?

There are many careers that involve bacteria in one way or another. One could be perfect for you. You might use bacteria to make foods. You might study bacteria to find ways to keep plants healthier for greater crop yield. You might discover a new way to use bacteria to clean up environmental pollution. You might research bacteria to cure diseases such as cancer or to stop the spread of bacterial pathogens. You might even be the one who figures out how to conquer the menace of drug-resistant bacteria.

If you decide to take one of these paths, you'll need a good working knowledge of biology, the study of living things. In the meantime, pay attention in science, math, English, history, and geography. Foreign languages will come in handy, too. Read a lot—books, newspapers, and magazines—and ask a lot of questions. When you get a little older, you might get a summer or after-school job in a cheese factory, a lab, or a hospital. Do some research in areas that interest you. Dig in and get to the bottom of it. Keep your eyes and ears open. Take notes, or keep a journal. Talk to people who work with bacteria—don't be shy, most people love talking about what they do.

Someday, kids might be asking you questions about your work with bacteria!

Final Project:
A Bacterial Safari

Bacteria are everywhere. They may be difficult to see without a microscope, but you can see and feel their effects in many ways. Let's grow bacterial colonies, the same way scientists do.

Materials:
- cotton swabs
- agar in petri dishes
- masking tape or labels
- pen or marker
- incubator: this can be made with a cardboard box with a light bulb suspended in it
- liquid antibacterial soap in a spray bottle
- notebook

Procedure:
1. Attach tape or a label to the outside of two petri dishes. Begin by putting your name and the date on the label, leaving room for other information.

2. Spray antibacterial soap on the surface of the agar in one of the petri dishes. Note that on the label of that dish.

3. Wipe a cotton swab on whatever you choose that you believe is teeming with bacteria. It could be a surface in your classroom, something in your lunch, water from the drinking fountain, or a specimen from your own body: your skin, your scalp, the inside of your mouth.

4. Next, rub the swab over the agar on one petri dish.

5. Repeat the wipe-rub from the same source on the other petri dish.

6. Label both dishes with the source of your specimen.

7. Cover the petri dishes and put them in the incubator. It's okay to stack the closed dishes on top of each other so there's room for a lot of petri dishes.

Optional: If there are enough petri dishes and your curiosity has taken over, take more samples. Just be sure you have two for each sample: one treated with antibacterial soap, one not. And be sure to label each clearly.

Observations: The next day, take your petri dishes out of the incubator. Look at them with your naked eye, and, if available, a magnifying glass or microscope.

What do you see? Write your observations in your notebook.

You might want to observe your cultures over the course of several days.

Conclusions: What do you think happened, and why?